Extravagance

Also by Irene Wilkie and published by Ginninderra Press
Love & Galactic Spiders

Irene Wilkie

Extravagance

Acknowledgements

Poems in this collection have appeared in *Yellow Moon, Taralla, Sun and Sleet, Five Bells, Blue Dog, Idiom 23, Australian Reader, Poetrix, Divan, All this Life, The Envelope Please, Leaving the Bow, Going Down Swinging, Mood Cumulus, Henry Lawson Festival of the Arts Anthology, Poetry Collaborations: Les Wicks, fourW eighteen, Broadkill Review USA, Surreal Wollongong, Tangents, Award Winning Australian Writing, Notes For Translators from 142 New Zealand and Australian Poets* and *Hoodworks*

Thanks to

The Kitchen Table Poets, Shoalhaven,
TAFE class conducted by Chris Mansell

Keith Wilkie for his endless cups of tea
my family
and Varuna for a Poetry Masterclass

Extravagance
ISBN 978 1 74027 812 6
Copyright © text Irene Wilkie 2013
Cover image: *road to culburra* (detail) by lea hawkins

First published 2013
Reprinted 2017

Ginninderra Press
PO Box 3461 Port Adelaide SA 5015
www.ginninderrapress.com.au

Contents

Behind the Sun	7
Heat	10
Webs	11
Improbable River Notes	13
Absurd	14
Chimera	16
Living Sculpture	17
Night Harbour	19
Mazurka	21
Darling	23
Rescue	24
Moonslide	26
Of Dandelions and Daisies	28
The Mountain Has Many Faces	31
The Humming	35
Daisy Chain	36
Looking Up	37
Silo	38
Child	39
Escapee	41
Cosmos	43
Creek Song	45
Daughter Painting Nails	46
Juggernaut	48
Tailspin	50
Dead World	51
Baby Boomers	52
Late Tourist	53
Crete	55
Opera	56

Two Score Years and Ten	57
Christmas Bush	59
Glass Graphic	61
Unchimed	62
Permanence	64
So Much Lightness	65
Slow Breathing	67
Flotilla	68
Cocoon	69
Acknowledgement details	72

Behind the Sun

The world keeps rolling and you are a focus   animate will
spun from light that has gone before   and you are alive with it
but what you learned last century is invalid   secure information
replaced   believable as video games

When truth moves it grows new surrounds   morphs into
    plasmas
different from the original first   second   third kind   complex
or simple   while the hole through the eye notes the changes
    converts them
into like and unlikely

slots them into boxes aligned against the vagaries of chance –
a crow measures the distance between itself and a sleepy skink or
the crow chooses a cockroach because the reckless thing moves
    too close
on its glossy clockwork legs

The void in the middle of understanding might never be filled –
the soul loops around it   under it   licks the outer skin   tests for
    validity
but never identifies the shape of it   yet pursues the purpose of
    seeking it out
wherever it lies –

perhaps in that place behind the sun where you watch comets
arrive on time
while errant meteors do not   where you consider fear in the face
    of fire
where you weigh the tangible against the nebulous   and wonder
if it matters

You observe the death of a butterfly   apply meaning to the last
   slow tremors
of the dying antennae   of wings still whole   a quivering
   a silent protest – and
the skink awakes uneaten   unclamps its jaw   swallows the
   hapless beetle
crawling between its toes

The crow chokes on the cockroach   spits out the spiny legs   and
   rests   if you look
at this in the light of the sun   the crow   the skink   the butterfly
   sheen their colour –
without the sun they are not like themselves   shadows
   invisible on
a black indifferent earth

At night colours die without light   except in your head where
   dreams are the colours
you own   playing real-life movies while you are inert   dreams
   spool movement
while you are paralysed   you hear yourself humming   wonder
   why you laugh
then realise what goes before

shapes what comes after designs to prevent it   you understand
   none of this at
the right time because the right time is always ahead of you or
   behind you
or nowhere at all   you must guess which time is right   what is
   right
and who says it might be

Is time a melting clock   sand running through glass   solar birth
    or death   does
time exist only when you and I exist and we think it   thinking
    the warm link of fingers   the wild beat of hearts?

You smile
The surprise is the surprise   you say   how busily we distract
    distraction
when we discover we make our own time – and we take it
    with us

Outside   in the half-light   the sunrise wind
rolls a gumnut down the tiles

Heat

fires a shot, a rivet shifts the veranda roof,
hosed-down creepers wet-barrier the air,
racquets, bicycles lean in shade.

We drink ginger beer, quell the body's steaming;
mother chatters – how cool the tennis courts
before the sun begins its burn.

My skirt is damp against my thighs, white shirt clings;
your eyes flick away like timid birds and I am aware –
the blond boy-fuzz, the robust chin, the temple rivulets.

Your voice quivers, not your own; you ask me
to the local picture show – Vivien and Clark.
My father nods approval, my mother smiles.

I think they like your honest look. I accept
the heart-hammer promise of closeness in the dark,
three delicious hours with you, holding hands.

You go home and I float inside
choosing what flimsy thing I'll wear.

The slow night
sends up a dusty moon –

father downs his beer
and mother chars the sausages.

Webs

And the glistening light is grass in the wind clicking
about our ears
we disturb small spiders in their flawless webs
the creek mutters somewhere   we lie on leaves
defiant
star shine vies with dawn light   each in suspension

Your coat warms me   night-morning sounds embrace
the eucalypts
as if they will live forever   like the earth
like the universe wrapped around us
throbbing
expanding   reaching down   bold on our eyelids

Our separate skins   voluptuous   enfold
interweave –
there is nothing but this consciousness
of valley moss   of mountain   coned to a point
spinning
swinging above our bodies   one to the other

We throw off the coats   the rugs   we laugh
astonished
because of the impermanence of things
the transient fragilities   improbabilities –
and say
this is all we can take from the world –

enough to keep us from the callous void
this joy
is worth the knowledge we might not have found
the answers   though we might have   but not all
and probably barely one

yet we dare
and our hearts tremble

Improbable River Notes

the flute
tensions the lips
woos as you play variations
on the lotus theme

how the long-fingered notes
bead web with sequin
shape indifferent silence
in rondoesque extravagance
define timpani of ballet shoe
thrum of orchestra

an unlikely song
dreaming whispered pine breath
improbable river notes

its trinket earth sounds
highlight the audacity of
pursed lips   live bones in skin

your music breathes   defying
solar hiss   the loneliness
of planets   inner hearts
dismiss the questions
and their answers –
how you charm the night

Absurd

You lure me into the valley,
territory of snake tongue,
spider foot, dingo eye.

You say
our molecules, our cells
share commonality
with marsupial mice,
river-gums,
orange-peel fungi.

You tell me
we recycle the same air,
taste the same rain
as the first hunters here,
baiting, trapping
the slow diprotodon.

I tell you as we stroll,
I could accept this oneness,
could forget the doubt,
and sit, with you,
hearing pebbles
shift and turn,
blue wrens dicker.

Then silently, a leech crawls,
finds my secret skin,
dissolves it in the circle of its mouth.

The rasping lip steals pleasure
without consent, sucks my blood,
like any common Dracula.
You light a match, burn the slimy thing,
not the act of connectedness
but you do it anyway.

The creature drops.
I stop the squirming with my boot,
grind my blood into the earth.

I stamp back to the track head
and you, behind me,
follow,
still babbling
your absurdities.

Chimera

She wakes   abstraction tugging at the cerebellum
a sentience in the fingertips   an anxiety of the hands
Her eyes shape the invisible   a wanton presence that isn't there
the unborn skin of it rolls as a child in its mother's belly

She speaks for its unfolding   for wild cries no one else can hear
tone ancestral   unlettered as the gilled rhythm of fish
the night glow of fungi   unreadable as a streak of storm
revolving in unformed state   a leech urgent as hunger

She entices into daylight this nebula   this nagging wasp   this
spider seeking   hermitage   a genie coveting sky   this
living thorn stops her breath   knots her space   interjects

She deciphers the snorting cry   the bucking strength –
lassoes the beast   tumbles it in sweat   rides   rides
on a rampage unspecified   wherever it must go

Trampled horizons   broken days   unveil the essence
unbridled impudence –
the impossible idea   testing its bones

Living Sculpture

All day the ferries rock   and charge the spray
across the bow;
green and crested waters match the rhythm
of the engine thrum inside.

All day the ferries lasso the wharf   salt rope
gunned like a noose
about each post   the strangled twisting chafe
drowns the swash of barnacles.

All day a sculptured girl tries her charm as travellers
rush to glass-walled canyon streets –
black-suited lemmings   footing it
ignore her studied stillness   the silent art
the hidden breath
the heart that begs for notice in the skill
of immobility
the pretence of marble skin   though it burns
of marble hair
of marble gown
that should not be stirring in the wind.

Her secret glance is shy and unobserved.
Yes, I am alive;
look, see this silent shift of hand
slow-rising wink of eye
and the beads of sweat on my upper lip –
are they not real?
All day she dreams of being somewhere else
but hears the meagre clink of coin –
stares ahead when children test for proof
of life or stone.

At five
she breaks her trance   the marble melts
from arms and legs   the rigid hands
discard the chiselled form.

She skips aboard the crowded ferry
its bouncing floor   she rolls and rocks
in perfect time to the engine-throb inside.

The orange-crested waters fade
the voices of the gull
then the harbour bridge lights up
in scintillating points
outdoes the stars

and night comes.

Night Harbour

The harbour is lit with sparks.

Plankton play
the beach
an x-ray graph
invites
the arch of spine
the dive into luminescence.

Arms split the water
glow
electric bubbles
trace the plume
the beat   the rolling slick.

Fluid light outlines
explores each hand
each finger   flares cold flame.

Eddies chase the pulse
the fizz   and shimmer –
our bodies
slice and slip

like incandescent seals
rising
to see a quarter-moon
dip pale ash in the fire-shot tide.

I slide about you
as fish and eel
gyrate their comet tails –
a neon choreography.

Without weight
without boundary
bright-edged   indestructible
we eclipse the stars.

Mazurka

High as rooftops
balloon men
wild with dance
clap tubular arms
in mechanical wind –
but they are not happy

Pumped vinyl bodies
fitful
convolute
protest at what they are –
candy-floss repetitions
of clowns like us –
swoop
bat the ground
tilt up and wrench
in frenzied spider-bite cadenzas
flap-slap hollow hearts
unable to escape

Tethered ad-spruiked mimics
titillate car-yard crowds
celebrate the victories
of local footie fans

Balloon men are not happy
although
they would have you think they are –

eyes bright-hot
black-lash outlined

hair   six vertical strips
each like the next one

Fixed laughs gape
fiercely weave
grasp at reasons
not to fear the night
when the pump clicks off –
when lights fade dim
and the world is flat

Darling

I've left something behind at your house but can't define what it is. I've looked at the things I brought back, checking what should be there, succeeding with all but one. That void is a question mark, a crook round my neck. The dot stays in place but despite what ploy I use to stretch and straighten the curve, it always springs back, latching me to the importance of settling irksome matters. I am locked in hesitation; why do I need these things; why do I carry them with me; why must I decorate them with songs and suns and moons until I have a chain of them. Somewhere I must call a halt before they bind me with their weight and I fall into a morbid state trying to classify them all. Perhaps this untitled thing is a friend telling me that it does not need to be quantified, that question marks should be treated to loving study. Perhaps it is a symbol, the dot being me squeezed into a tiny place and you, the unrelenting hook that keeps the dog in, or a sheep. Perhaps this object is not untitled but unrecognised as the link between a gate and a fence. Whether to retrieve or not, now or if at all, becomes clearer when I consider what I have left behind your locked doors. I am enabled. My scalp need not hang from your belt. Entrapment of an unknown or even known quantity is not my kind of suspense. My question marks should be deleted after reading.

Rescue

It's a mini aberration, a quick sidestep,
delicious as intrigue,
entrapment on a blustery day at a market in the suburbs.
Trestle-table bric-a-brac
holds treasure I must have. What delight is hidden here
for nothing but a dollar?

The spruiker's call, It's blowing like a banshee,
hang in there everyone,
accelerates the salivation, windfall scent,
the tensing of hot fingers
locked on luck; the eye scans the trembling stalls.

There must be a bargain here, charmed amulet,
scarab, locket, ruby thing,
wrapped, unwrapping, value overlooked
by nearly everyone.
Dusty masks and hats lift off, ceramics rock –

I play my act,
the poses of intention, the holding to the light
wasted on the wind.
Damn the westerly. The thief steals time, howls us down.

My chances are diminishing –
and frantic, I choose before the whole damned business
hoons away.
I grab a greenstone owl, for its symmetry of feathered eye.
So little to pay
for a witching head, feet clamped against
catastrophe.
Beside it, a rosy leprechaun grins at the joke
on all of us.

I take the two, expecting, on inspection,
cracks in a beak,
in a painted shoe, a yielding of the skin,
a thinning of the breakable.

A foolish gamble this but surely something must
be strong enough to rescue each of us –
possibly a superglue,
       a superman,
       a super-human hero –
the cement against unravelling?
Possibly,
       possibly.

Moonslide

she is not content
to paint the city –
not content
with silvered surfaces
of balcony and wall
tower and street
courtyard tile and vine

she asks too much
my love and just like you
flows in airy flimsiness
through open windows
across the floor
shines her borrowed light
searches my face
measures the mood –

she thinks she can banish unease
and calm me   soothe with her touch
in pools of still half-night
my eyes   lids low
observe
her smooth advance
the gliding luminosity
she exudes
to prove that she can
charm   even though
I know
she plans to vanish

like you   my sweet
she chooses the perfect time
as she lifts shadow
from the darkest corner
the clicked-off lamp
the bedside table
carved lilies in the vase
when her presence bathes
the room   attunes my pulse
toward her clear intention

that she   like you
will steal
wordless
brushing light   gentle
against my skin
until I acquiesce   that her gaze
like yours
binds with the twine of witchery
and the heart seeks no escape

Of Dandelions and Daisies

You hold a finger to the wind   seek a guide to the familiar   the places
the faces lit with skies of yesterday   childhood summers bursting full of hope and cleverness.

Where are the leather-bound truths   lost timbres of forgotten choirs the angel chants?
None remain except as tenuous threads   as repeated wormy words sung a thousand years ago.

The earth rolls you in the ache of leadlight windows   of dusk misted beneath the pines
of the yellowness of daisies   of dandelion   the white of lily   of thistledown.

Time betrays while you decipher what is known or not   afraid to learn the unknowable
the possibility of understanding the impassive eye of a universe

the humming of mindless noise that does not know   does not care if you
love or live   that your head is heavy as stone   that your fingers probe for certainties out of reach.

You are not meant for any part of such a deal   giddy with the rush of time
you are a bee avoiding a web   a wren escaping the eagle   and you have never learned how.

With nothing to hold on to   you discover something small   something
that shines through gaps   something   blinking like a warm brown bird
shyer than shadow;

whatever it wants to say fades in   fades out   trickling only fragments
of what you need   you guess it is never too late to begin the search for more
and always too early to end it.

Whenever you might begin   there is regret you have not noticed earlier –
you need lines to be circular   a never-ending chance to gather time for entry
somewhere along a circumference

whose end is a beginning   hidden   and you must find it   you suspect
a centrifuge   spun blood congealed   the paste applied to mend the retina;
the eye's sweep

restored from distortion   simply as viewing unadorned skin measures
the distance from the tip of your nose to where your feet are discovered
stumbling into stellar dust.

The earth rolls you   like tumbleweed   brittle in the solar wind.
Let it spin its mountain tops   quicken cataclysmic chasms
   threaten
the eternal threat.

You hold a dandelion   a daisy   touch a sunsplit shadow –
how they sweetly glow.

The Mountain Has Many Faces

1. Abyss

On the lip of the precipice, beside the falls,
an up-draught ripples wattle,
scents the air.

You lean, I see you dreaming –
less than substance, unharnessed,
you wing rainbows.

Tongue untethered, you catapult your call
against the orange rock, the strata lines,
the sly edges.

The echoes climb and swell, climb and drop
and in the moment before they die,
stir tall bloodwoods
on the valley floor –
a sea of olive green.

I watch you toss a wattle sprig
far out beyond the wire.

The yellow spray
glides deep-eyed distances –
and drowns.

2. Icy Cinema

To stand at the head of the valley
to look out into space where
ice-clouds crystal on the wind
glistening the first approach of winter's
cinematography –
to face new snow sweeping
the high air so fast we clench our fists
ready to meet it on a stark cliff edge –
to see the yellow sun fire this tongue of wrath
seething toward us   dank underbelly growling
through the arms of ironbark –
to see the hawk bank and turn before the gale
the waterfall curl its mist in long streamers
of errant draught
is to shout that we are the only ones
in this place   on this spur
to greet the snow's first drum roll –
the only ones embracing
the gold   the white
the purple   the black
about to wrap us in breath so sharp
the freeze will be as flame.

3. Two worlds at once

Sandstone,
strata interlaced with shale,
rock-set ripples
moulded by an ancient beach,
a shallow bay, a million aeons old.

Though here the bush is dry,
though here are wind-topped trees,
though no ocean laps the track,
we finger sea-shaped things
in midday heat, above the plain –
everywhere, the evidence.

We measure dip, slip, fracture zone,
imagine how the sea lilies died,
how fluted shellfish, winged, intact,
were trapped inside their stony tombs,
how manta rays were fixed in ballet,
jellyfish in print, complexities in silica.

We hear our blood
pulse arteries like a tide,
hear wallaby and lizard leap,
hear the spinebill cease its hover
flaring up from mountain bloom.

Your eyes reflect, as mine,
primeval sea, wind-washed land.

How similar are their voices.
How they play the ear.

4. Silver

The mountain tells its secrets –
the friendship with the silky oak,
the whispers between them
of lovers stealing time,
the gentle tones of promise,
the night chords the wind makes
gliding through the canopies,
the sleeping sounds,
the slide of silver.

The Humming

Sapphire body   mosaic wings
skim bright water   the dragonfly
skirts the spitting fish   the stork
the slanted looms of light

split shadows   the traps
of afternoon   rapid water beads
sticky silk above clear pools
at the feet of giant river oak

She avoids the dragon tongue
the swift release   outwits with grace
the child with net and line
the bent and jagged pin

She traces the depth of nectar wells
notes mud's treachery
tracks the upper   the lower air
the humming
flags this stretch of pond

She owns a fluted world of reeds
for a season   no reason
except perhaps the flight
joyously begun
fearlessly lived
surprisingly ended –

and not one footprint

Daisy Chain

Wattle
colours the last winds of winter,
wakens bees into urgency –
the solstice passing.

A slow repeat
unfolds the golden whistler's return,
the shearwater's southern flight,
the cockatoo's bob and bow,
the chatter and the duel.

The earth's turning
pulls us from the house.
Aroused by longer days,
arms bare, feet unshod,
we dream of daisy chains,
the petals on the skin
and hunger for the warm air
melting icy syllables
on the tongue.

I see you pulse new energy,
calling me.

We search the daisy fields,
discover swollen buds –
the promised bloom
enough.

Looking Up

In blue-etched chaos
thin fingers brush the sun,

dark hands offer
the unfurled leaf bud,

perfumed magnolia,
silhouette of bird,

the ballooning
of cicada skirl.

In a silence between,
the phone rings

and I hear you,
also singing.

Silo

on familiar landscape
a strange sunrise
probes mist
in the ghost gums
cones in the she-oak
muted spaces widening
in beaded foliage

cows stand belly-deep
in invisibility

a horse rubs his back
against ethereal wattle

the feather-capped notes of wrens
fade
against bull-throated frogs

fence posts   disembodied
trap light along the wire
sun-edged tussocks blink

like a morning lighthouse
sea drifting
the silo reflects
borrowed gold
waiting for the wheat

Child

I am
curved as a clef,
full blown.

I am in tune
with the world,
hear the unsuspected melodies,
the timpani of rapids
a rhetoric
I've never heard,
jazz
at the feet of eucalypt.

Blossom swells;
bees, relentless
in the fretwork on blue,
thrum, busier than they
ever were before.

I carry
a growing list,
small miracles
to recount
to this new child.
How can I remember
each discovery?

Will I forget
to tell him how
the wind
sighs in paper leaves, how
the laboured flight
of beetles drones the air?

Will I forget
to tell him how
the laughter
in his father's heart,
brought the singing into mine?

When this baby
stands and walks,
if I take him
by the hand,
let him teach me
more delight
in each first-time marvel
reflected from his eyes,

I will not forget.

Escapee

She is on the cliff edge,
notes the distance to the sea,
the clacking, the sucking.

Wind-whip slaps
hair into her mouth,
needles grit against her skin,
whines in her ears,
tugs and wrenches
at her grip on broken wire,
broken fence – her bloodless nails
cunning with stealth.

The child, centre of her eye,
squats small, curious on a jutting spur,
an unsafe place, a sky-bound place.

Dear God, don't let him see me.
She stretches
every bone, every tendon,
creeps smooth as any fox –
as if this is a natural thing.

Don't let him move.
Her arms are not yet round his body,
not yet as she approaches,
pushing down the fear,
breath locked in vacuum.

Don't let him take one step –
She edges closer,
ready to clasp his curiosity,
his fearless promise,
the not-yet-unfolded life

and he turns his head,
laughs at her playing
some new, delicious joke,
some riotous peek-a-boo.
Her heart
is belting through her chest
as she sees him stand and totter,
mouth shaping, Bird, bird.

She springs,
grabs his shirt,
wraps his wriggling squeal
in the steel of her, the tears of her.

Come, young man.
It's time for tea.

He peeps at her face.
Can we have egg?

She thinks
how fragile his dear head.

If you're good, she says.

Cosmos

I expect
the mountain to melt,
the sea to thirst,
the incineration of sky.
I walk sharp blades,
my heart certain
this earth cannot last.

There is nowhere to go.
No cave,
no jungle
can bury my fear
for the unsuspecting children.

They are the flesh, the sinew
of my songs –

through my fingers
art becomes the soul
and artful I must keep
away the viper's sting.

I show each child my book,
the syntax
as brace
against a lethal world
but their eyes flick past
my candle.
There is nothing between us,
yet everything.

Like monkeys
their voices chatter
to a roofless wind
that must return
to the cosmic void.

I take cover in the hoot of an owl.

Creek Song

for Belinda

There is a dub-dub-dub on two notes
the base-line
of a cadence
>   rising
>   drumming on every rock
to the top of the discordant octave
the twang
a flurry of surge
brown foam slick
>   scours the banks
>   searches out the anxious roots
of giants that know
they can't live forever
placidly lean
until they fall
become reluctant bridges
>   for vampires and goblins
>   witches and wombats

and fourteen-year-old kids on bicycles
voices and bells two octaves higher –
blending in daredevil harmony.

Daughter Painting Nails

Framed in unbraided hair
you spread your fingers,
paint your nails Talon Red.

With the precision of
Michelangelo,
the daring of Picasso,
naked intent affronts
decorum's cause,
brush-strokes rebellion.

Unaware the ancestry of fingernails
precedes time as claws,
you hold them wet like blood
splitting the air
with busyness.

You flaunt them like weapons,
dragons on the edge of change,
scorching reason.

The child is becoming woman.

You might agree to listen
or you might shake your head
but I must try
some sort of gesture
against that terrible red,
before you leave.

So imminent a flight
to freedom's web
spills my question
from trembling lips,

    My darling,
        what would you think
            about Rose Pink?

Juggernaut

Logos conspire
on chicken boxes
flicked under bridges.

At the clogged waterfall
rapids try to sing along
and jiggle a plastic spoon.

Between stepping stones
jutting cartons trip my feet.
I crash in
with battered nuggets
burger buns and salad.

TV jingles chime
saggy wrappings
round my fingers
slippery with chicken fat.
The creek flushes me
into the river maligned
in sludge and free Coke bottles
maladjusted line up
to cheer my soggy bleat.

Lips compressed
I spill out of the river mouth.

Someone
has secreted dioxin
on the bottom of the harbour.
There is a hum of cover-up.

I escape into the open sea.
Piped bubbles six ks out
buoy my flesh
not sweet enough for sharks.

Supermarket trolleys
marinate
in deep briny ravines
blue as grottoes –
and I can sluice
in red drainage
from science-based whale-steak ships.

Perhaps they will hose me down.

Tailspin

disturbed and bothered
the sky blathers
the unexpected
snowfall in Darwin
heatwave in Antarctica
sends icebergs too far north
frightens the dreaming yachts
into fearful vigilance

no one recalls weather like this
all at once
and in the wrong places

the sky strums taut wires
pelts singing nails
adds screaming as experiment

we swarm
around the warming pot
that frogs boil in

jungles slip into desert
sand spiders spin grit webs
pull stony shields
across their backs

and concrete-studded landscapes
dream meteors of extinction

Dead World

In response to *Life Is Still* (oil on board) by Joan Meats

What planets
have gone before
this voiceless relic
framed in possibility,
bred for harvest?

Did men
carve their niche here –
did their children's children
bleed the soil,
poison the air?

What ruthless sun burned
flesh from bones,
purpose from precision?

What eye remained to mourn
the ear of stone?

Baby Boomers

Grateful that the leading paradigm
of existence
steams ahead with no gaps
where someone
is missing at the table
set with two chairs,
marmalade jam, toasted weeties
afloat in low-fat milk,
our hearts waltz
on with easy joy,
not caring
what the finite number is
already clocked
by that metronome in the sky.

We discover talents hitherto
uncovered,
projects needing more time
than scrolls ahead.
Enthused we drool
cool achievement, paint like
Grandma Moses,
write a shorter *Gone With The Wind*.
In our residual
span of years, we cavort
tauter than tortoises,
quicker than quicksilver,
sparkle expertise
until the very, very last minute.

Late Tourist

We were late in the season, tourists following
the end of summer, leaving England, winding
through Paris
and in a southern French cave,
we discovered
rock-carved neolithic bulls,
before the winter closures.

In Greece, an amphitheatre echoed songs
of ancient longing;
in a *plaka*, rude waiters flicked contempt,
the climate growing colder

but nothing matched the simple meal,
feta cheese and bread,
olives, fish and greens on the less-known
western lava rim of Santorini.

Two couples left the ferry, wandered off.
We were the late, late tourists, solo in his warm café,
the food on offer ready for a crowd.

Like family he served us, this eager man,
his wife peeping, her mouth set tight.
We wished there were more than two of us.

He didn't ask us for much,
not enough to balance
the steamed aroma of welcome,
the riotous-coloured choices, the spiced tomato,
the pilaf we wanted to eat but couldn't.

In shy English, he wished us the best
of the season
as if it was just beginning.

Outside, the day had lost its early bite,
we climbed back aboard the ferry
and our host closed the shop.

Crete

    at the sea wall
      a man in thongs
        spears an octopus
          for lunch
            flicks it inside out
              trims off the useless bits
              carries it upside down
            trails across the road
                a scream in ink and blood

Opera

This train scrapes with voice –
a scratchy violin   a base bassoon
with attitude
    not petulant
    but urgent   flighty chat
down and up the scales
    staccato down the slopes
    legato up
dragging weights too much for it
moderato through black tunnels
like water over deepest channels
and on the flats
allegretto clatter
swells the monologue.
Hot silver paint
fake velvet seats
are there for show   it says
the grind and grime will wear away the shine
    jolt by jolt   and can by can
    so will graffiti   the slam of doors
    your hurried feet
    heavy the heart
but what the hell
    music is the thing
    and the talk talk talk
        talk talk talk
        talk

Two Score Years and Ten

Fractious as colts in grass after rain
free of stables and barriers
they push out of every pore
the breath of promise.

She comes prancing into his life
eyes leading   body arched
unbridled   seeking
warmth and natural intention.

Her hair blankets out the cold
her voice quells his fear –
the convention –
the everyday of toil and progeny.

He doesn't care where he is
what he is and for what slab of time
the journey   he doesn't care
while she savours the sky thing
the blossom thing   the whispered thing.

The offspring come   soon go
with their own intentions –
their inventions of filial love.

He discovers his hair is wearing thin –
and she is rounder
than an autumn moon.

The city gallops   swallows the sunny fields
corrals them in   traffic champs
at the bottom of the garden.

For fifty seasons he has asked
as if there is a deity
that he last the days with her –
he   astonished   slow-flanked
still dreaming.

Christmas Bush

Our Christmas bush is turning red –
white blossom dropped
from each bright calyx, separates
as an accidental afterthought.

I cut the stems in armfuls,
decorate on Christmas Eve
as I remember
those who did the same
with homespun gifts
and ritual belief
that nothing would be different
despite the talk of war

but spiders crawl
the leaves of Christmas bush.

Forced to comprehend
time bites,
people disappear,
the child becomes
the woman glimpsing ghosts
of eyes and lips,
blurred among red sprays –
every year
a brief return.

I look up
as children run into the room,
seeming not to notice
anyone but each other.

We fill vases, loop paper bells,
thread tinselled stars
and I hold
new images for old —

something of theirs,
borrowed.

Glass Graphic

You hear the thud on the windowpane
and know the sound:
some bird   tricked by reflection
mistakes illusion
for reality   leaves its mark on glass –
one drop of blood
a dusty body print
etched in feathers.

Wingtips are spread
claws bunched   beak caught
wide in the shock
of arrested flight –

a portrait
of unexpected death
backlit by
afternoon transparency.

You look through
while the image remains
before
new rain obliterates
the sad silly thing.

Unchimed

Her wind chimes are hyphenated melody   uncomposed
interrupted snatches of what could be   could have been
might be   the breath is breathless   breathing   tries to
interweave the interplay   the waves   and flurries with

the thoughtless wind   puffing and probing about
the eaves   eavesdropping   listening to what might
eventuate   what is   and what is not   invents sequences
never fulfilled   spills errant notes   shrill   unstrung

as they are   her ears grown deaf to them   won't listen
wrapped   as she is   in private hummings   brackets of
crotchets   mounting and climbing the mind   looped through
boxes   ironed memories folded in cells   the smell of naphthalene

She unwraps an aging parcel   brown paper sweet with
ancient lavender significant as incense   she twitches her nose
always sniffing in the search for permanence   bright images
leap each time   from faded silks bound in ribboned memory

She sweeps away mouse leavings   tweezers a paper silverfish
wonders why she hears no squeaks   no cockroach scurries
no whisker rubbings   no whisper of long delicate feelers
or cricket chirrups   beetle clicks   she questions why

why she can't find a tongue to match the words in her   why
she is wandering a cage   why the clangour   the piping   why
the whipping   the crescendo of regret smites inside her head until
full of it   she finds no comfort as the solitary target audience
She rejects the jangled cursing   erratic jargon beat   foots the circled
rooms   steps close and closer   out the door where the madness
clamours in   she grips   rips down the wind chimes   the ringing
the incessant incompletions   the endless clang of middlesong

They are unloosed   stilled as rusted reeds
and she hears herself again   her soft breath

From the wind's true voice   she retrieves forgotten notes
and humming   weaves her own melody

Permanence

yes   I'm over it
the death of my mother
doesn't clamp my throat so much
now we have walled her
behind a plaque   bright
as a copper morning

I think of her
in sudden places   the usual
strangers see me remember
her paper hands
speak the words
and this is my eldest daughter

the space she leaves
follows my ear
an audio disc
plays her voice
hold me   it is dark

on a nebulous screen
I embrace her arms   and wrists
I stroke her frightened face
surprised at pain
she tries to keep from me

I hold her
and she sleeps

So Much Lightness

So much lightness and breath exploding,
so much clarity of raindrop and dew;
there is too much flap and flurry of feather
to hear the hyacinths.

It's the lorikeet's chatter and shriek,
the guttural screech from a brush-tipped tongue;
it's the claw, the beak, the tapering wing,
dazzle-rich in rainbow.

It's the crowd of them, the interweave
the jostling, the biting, the severance –
such madness in the bloodwood blossom,
the filaments fall like rain.

The pink serenade of azalea, of rose,
lament of forget-me-not are quelled,
beaten deep into silence beneath
the careless cacophony.

Stripped branches, twigs, gumnuts litter,
pelt the half-buried hyacinths
and when the honey feast runs dry
the flocks hurtle off to the next.

They have gone; there is peace, enough
to unearth my exotics, release them from
the tumbled shadow, the heaped debris
of bacchanalia.

The lorikeets will raid again,
maybe next year or maybe not –
over the rise, a chainsaw whines,
a bloodwood falls;

someone new talks about a garden.

Slow Breathing

Cotton-cloud day,
wet earth,
the shine of rock
are mine again –
I breathe
a slower beat.

On yellow dunes
salt grass writes the wind
and the tidal march drums stone,
clatters pebbles in the pools,
veils the cliff in white.

Foam flies its flag,
seaweed strays like hair
and my face is wet.

In the mornings,
familiar, light-washed,
      wind-tipped things
      change.
I walk with dawn birds
searching for the difference.

Flotilla

jellyfish
suspended
at
dusk
as if they are
the only true life form
in ocean space

drift
with fluorescent certainty
afloat
domed and clustered
as they always are

undulate
threads of stinging barbs
play the lazy currents
display the sway
the hidden
unsuspected capability

of dance

Cocoon

This is safe   isn't it   immured   hidden in shadow tweaked with light
hidden among   hidden by ghost gums   by parrots on braided twigs woven
streaked in uppermost sheaths of canopy   in this safe walling this native forest
you think like the apes not yet men   like the woodcutter not yet treeless
think and believe there is nothing to shatter the peaceful air drifting on the skin
no reason for fear   you deny you hear any kind of hiss   near or distant

This is peace   isn't it   the closing of the door with click and lock the sigh of
breath shifting motes from clock and bench   picture windows frame the room
purpose laid out in blinds   in carpet loops   the uncurled toe a mood as if
the easing is proof that all this existence is meant to be   can never be disrupted
disarrayed   discontinued when you know it could but not yet not now
not here in this familiar space   this cocoon of designer plan and everlasting paint

This is living　isn't it　the tap of feet on linoleum　the pop of gas
　　the cheer of
hot roast lamb　cool drinks iced with mint　clothes washed in
　　lavender　this sleeping
in silk　while in the roof a snake rustles vertebrae　and some
　　kind of spotted frog
bops in weeds　the seeds of dreams wing in from the stars to
　　charm your view　to prove
your trust that this must surely go on forever　when you wake
　　you say it may be true as
breakfast boils its egg　you shower in sweet warm water
　　and the radio fast-talks the hour

This is paradise　isn't it　the clouded sun fans silver rays　the
　　baby takes a step
the garden sprouts frilled lettuce　the car hums easy　you
　　applaud this scented day　this is
joy in your exultant voice and you don't care if it can't last or
　　hold or stretch out through
time like the yellow road　you don't care　you clasp it now　all
　　of it　the lemons and
the vinegar　the caramel and the chocolate　you tease out juices
　　the piquant taste builds
fills your cocoon　fuses the giddy dance with filtered breeze
　　the usual radiant thing

This is a dance   isn't it   across your rooms   across your foolish
   brow   like thought
choosing   fingers touching the first spring leaves of the indoor ivy
   the wall shapes cast through glass
this is escape   a connivance of the mind to ignore dark
   certainties with a stamp of leather boot
a prance of satin shoe   you skip   sing of everything   you will
   not cry unless you must
for loss   the seep of it   the drip of it in far corners
   beneath your mossy eaves   night shadows cling
      but in the morning
      there is riot   there is revelry
      and the parrots chatter into light
      again

Acknowledgement details

Behind the Sun: *The Envelope Please*, FAW National Literary Awards 2007
Webs: *Sun and Sleet*, NSW Poets' Union Anthology 2008
Improbable River Notes: (published as Extravagance) *Five Bells*, Summer 2006–07; *Broadkill Review* USA 2007
Absurd: *Five Bells*, Autumn 2006
Chimera: *Australian Reader*, 2007
Living Sculpture: *Henry Lawson Festival of the Arts Anthology*, (Grenfell) 2011; *Award Winning Australian Writing* 2011, Melbourne Books
Night Harbour: *Divan*, Issue 7 2009 (online)
Mazurka: *Five Bells*, Festival Double Issue 2009
Darling: *Blue Dog*, Vol. 7 No. 13 2008
Rescue: *Idiom 23*, Vol. 19 2007
Moonslide: *Five Bells*, Vol. 17 No. 3 2010
The Humming: *Yellow Moon*, Issue 17 2005
Silo: (published as Waking) *Poetrix*, Issue 28 May 2007
Child: *All This Life*, FAW Shoalhaven Anthology 2007
Escapee: *Henry Lawson Festival of the Arts Anthology* 2009
Cosmos: *Mood Cumulus*, Central Coast Poets NSW 2006
Creek Song: *Poetrix*, Issue 37, Western Women Writers 2011
Juggernaut: *Going Down Swinging*, Issue 26 2008
Tailspin: *Poetrix*, Issue 28 2007
Baby Boomers: *fourW* eighteen, Wagga Writers Centre 2007
Late Tourist: *Australian Reader*, 2006
Opera: *Hoodworks*, Well Sprung Productions (C. Mansell) 2012
Two Score Years and Ten: *Leaving the Bow*, Central Coast Poets 2008
Slow Breathing: (published as Space) *Poetry Collaborations*, Les Wicks 2006

Dead World: (published as Life Is Still) *Surreal Wollongong,* Wollongong City Gallery 2008

Glass Graphic: *Taralla,* Issue 4 2005

Permanence: *Yellow Moon,* Issue 17 2005

Cocoon: *Notes for Translators from 142 New Zealand and Australian Poets* 2012, ed. C. Kelen, Association of Stories in Macao and Cerberus Press

www.ingramcontent.com/pod-product-compliance
Lightning Source LLC
Chambersburg PA
CBHW062153100526
44589CB00014B/1814